How To Draw Comic Animals

Illustrations and Instructions by Walt Trag

Materials

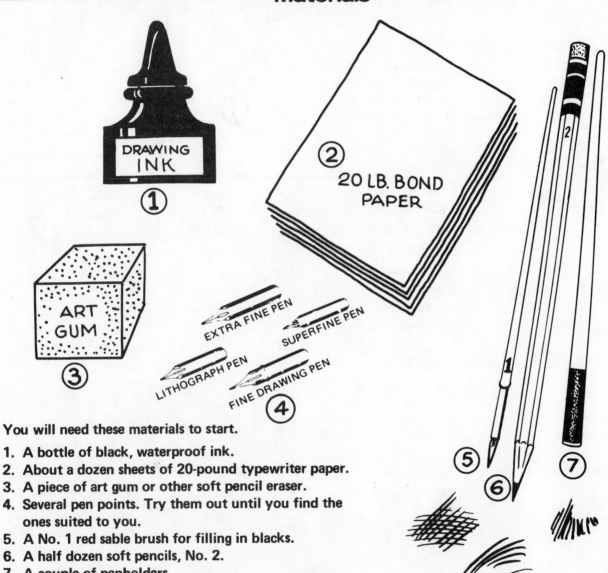

You will need these materials to start.

1. A bottle of black, waterproof ink.
2. About a dozen sheets of 20-pound typewriter paper.
3. A piece of art gum or other soft pencil eraser.
4. Several pen points. Try them out until you find the ones suited to you.
5. A No. 1 red sable brush for filling in blacks.
6. A half dozen soft pencils, No. 2.
7. A couple of penholders.

You will also need a pencil sharpener. Any kind will do.

For a drawing board, you can use a small sheet of masonite or wall board, 18 inches by 22 inches. This can be bought at your local lumberyard.

Practice pen and ink lines like this until you can draw them easily.

YOUTH PUBLICATIONS / THE SATURDAY EVENING POST COMPANY

Copyright © 1978 by The Saturday Evening Post Company, Indianapolis, Indiana.
ISBN 0-89387-573-2

Bugs

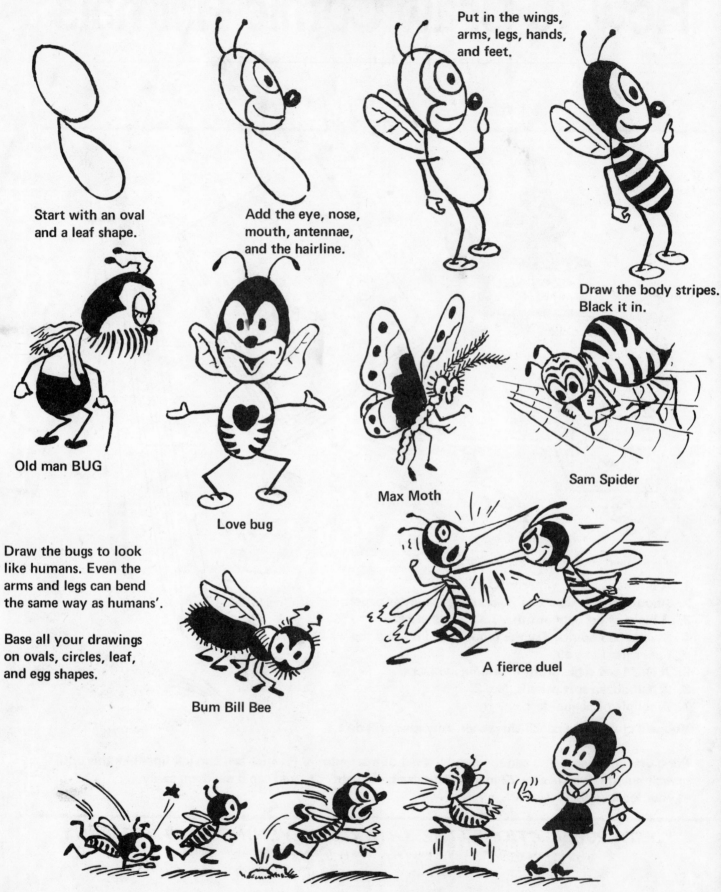

Start with an oval and a leaf shape.

Add the eye, nose, mouth, antennae, and the hairline.

Put in the wings, arms, legs, hands, and feet.

Draw the body stripes. Black it in.

Old man BUG

Love bug

Max Moth

Sam Spider

Draw the bugs to look like humans. Even the arms and legs can bend the same way as humans'.

Base all your drawings on ovals, circles, leaf, and egg shapes.

Bum Bill Bee

A fierce duel

Mama Bug and the kids

4

Mice

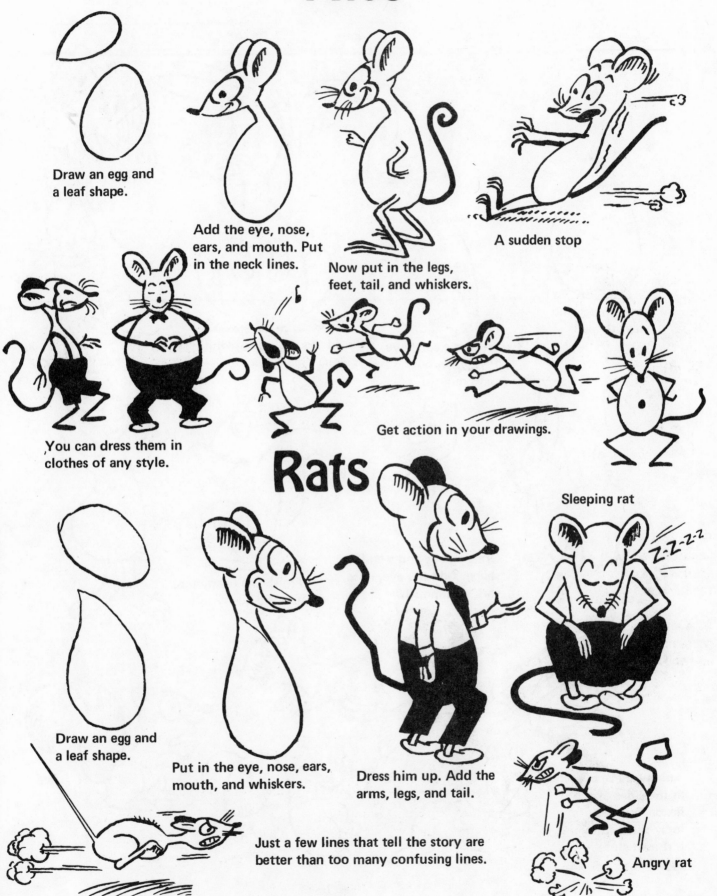

Draw an egg and a leaf shape.

Add the eye, nose, ears, and mouth. Put in the neck lines.

Now put in the legs, feet, tail, and whiskers.

A sudden stop

You can dress them in clothes of any style.

Get action in your drawings.

Rats

Draw an egg and a leaf shape.

Put in the eye, nose, ears, mouth, and whiskers.

Dress him up. Add the arms, legs, and tail.

Sleeping rat

Just a few lines that tell the story are better than too many confusing lines.

Angry rat

5

Rabbits and Squirrels

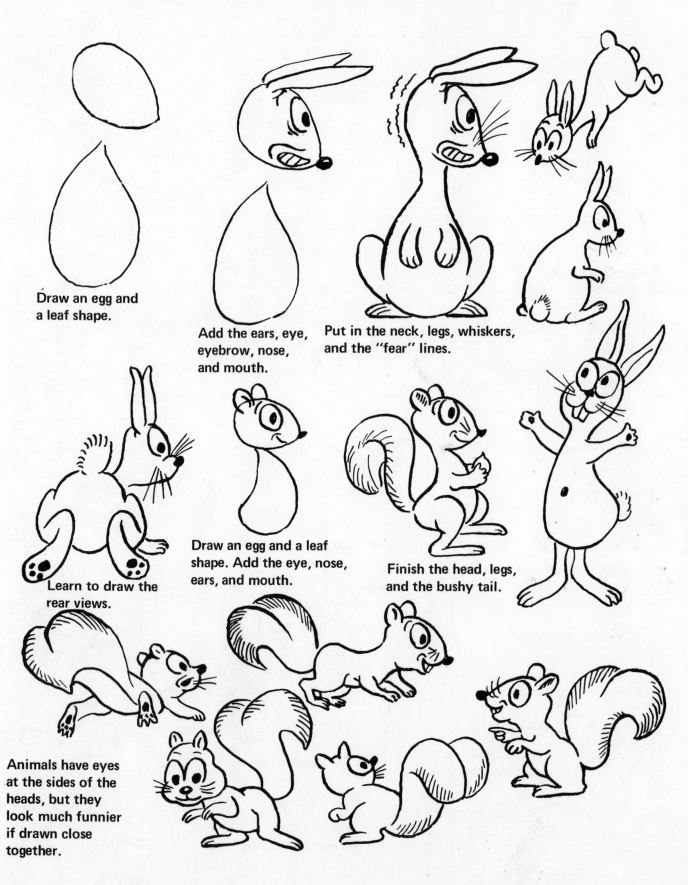

Draw an egg and a leaf shape.

Add the ears, eye, eyebrow, nose, and mouth.

Put in the neck, legs, whiskers, and the "fear" lines.

Learn to draw the rear views.

Draw an egg and a leaf shape. Add the eye, nose, ears, and mouth.

Finish the head, legs, and the bushy tail.

Animals have eyes at the sides of the heads, but they look much funnier if drawn close together.

Cats and Kittens

Start with a circle and a leaf shape.

Add the ears, eye, nose, mouth, and the whiskers.

Finish the body. Put in the legs and tail. Black it in.

Pretty puss

Surprised cat

Angry cat

Put human expressions on all the animals and make them act like humans.

They are easier and faster to draw that way.

Use plenty of extreme action.

Whenever possible, use plenty of black spots. This will "pep" up the drawings and make them stand out.

Dogs and Pups

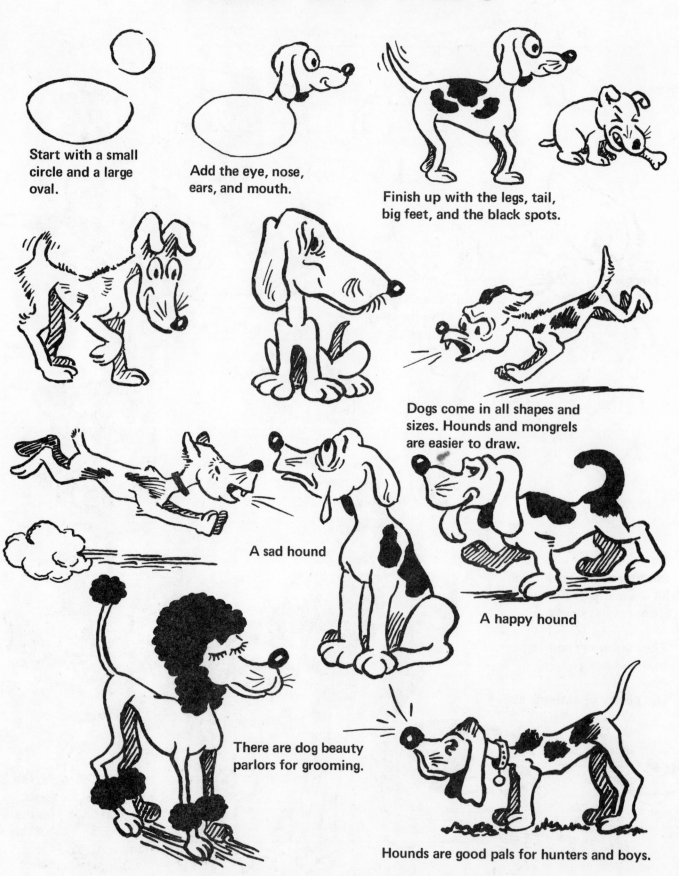

Start with a small circle and a large oval.

Add the eye, nose, ears, and mouth.

Finish up with the legs, tail, big feet, and the black spots.

Dogs come in all shapes and sizes. Hounds and mongrels are easier to draw.

A sad hound

A happy hound

There are dog beauty parlors for grooming.

Hounds are good pals for hunters and boys.

The dachshund is a real l - o - n - g dog.

Pups are always cute and lovable.

Bloodhounds look
sad and sleepy.
They are very gentle.

Fierce dog

Timid dog

9

More Dogs

A Saint Bernard may weigh up to 200 pounds.

Draw a small circle and a large oval.

Well-fed pup

Finish it up like this.

The Mexican Chihuahua may weigh less than a pound.

Greyhounds are built for speed.

Half-starved stray dogs eat when they can. They're very ragged and pitiful.

Bulldogs are tough-looking. They are very friendly.

Horses

Start with two ovals. Add the lines for the legs, ears, tail, and the hooves.

Put in the face. Finish the tail.

Add the mane and forelock. Finish the legs and hooves. Put in the black spots.

"Boy, am I tired!"

Surprised

Frisky horse

Happy

"Let me out of here!"

Good eating

11

Mules

Draw two ovals as shown here.

Mules and donkeys have long ears.

Finish it the same way as the horse. Make him look surprised.

Donkeys and Colts

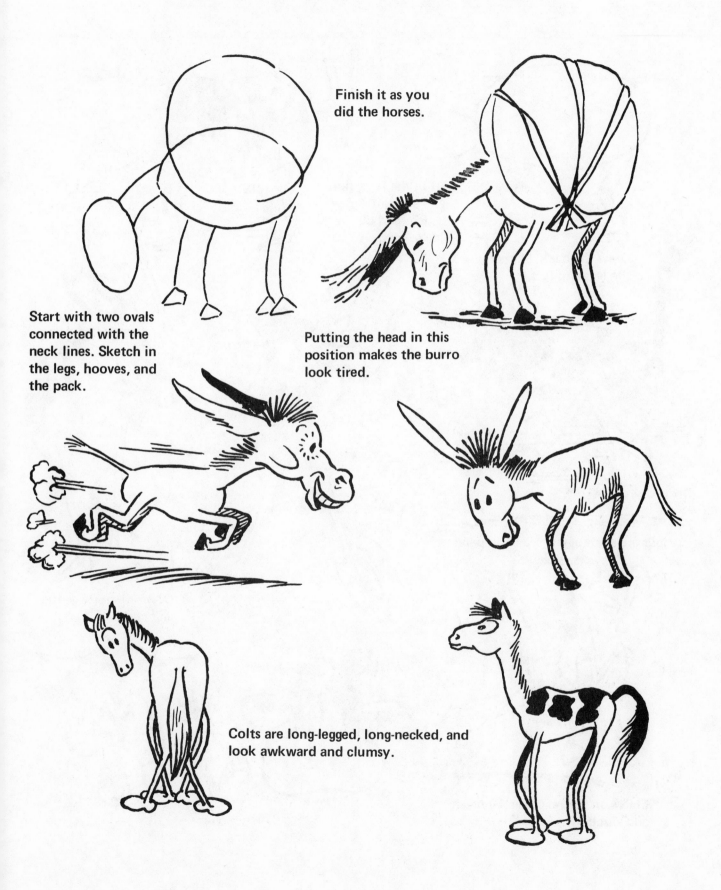

Finish it as you did the horses.

Start with two ovals connected with the neck lines. Sketch in the legs, hooves, and the pack.

Putting the head in this position makes the burro look tired.

Colts are long-legged, long-necked, and look awkward and clumsy.

Cows and Bulls

Draw the ovals. Sketch in the legs and feet.

Put in the face, horns, ears, and tail. Draw the legs and put in the black spots.

Bulls are sometimes mean and ugly.

Cows are quite gentle and curious.

Steers on the range can be mean and stubborn.

More Cows

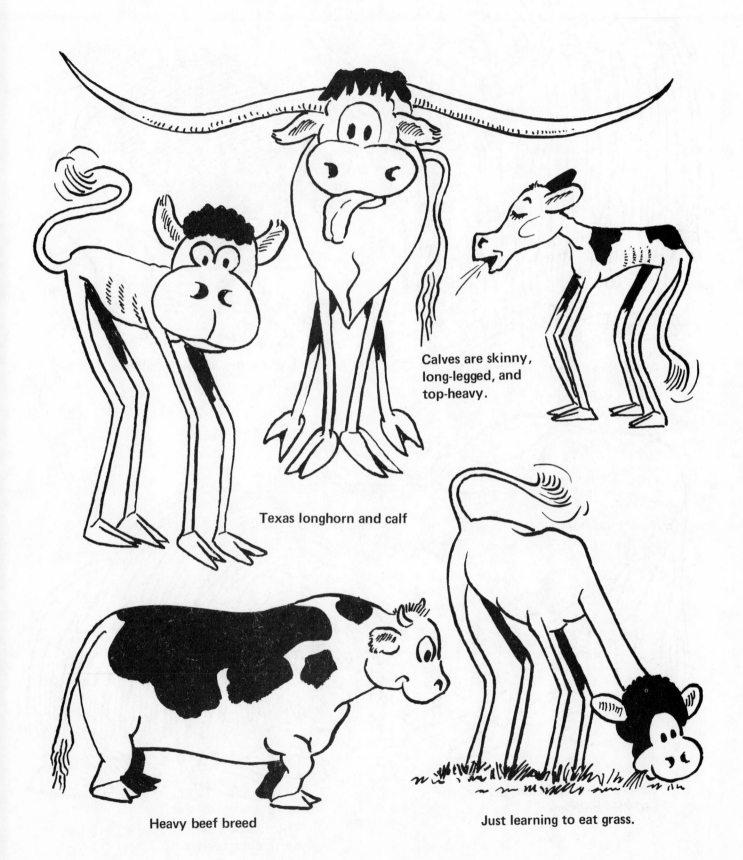

Calves are skinny, long-legged, and top-heavy.

Texas longhorn and calf

Heavy beef breed

Just learning to eat grass.

Yak-Bison-Water Buffalo-Musk-Ox

Yaks live in Tibet.

The bison is the American buffalo.

Water buffalo are found in Asia and the Philippines.

The musk-ox lives in the north polar regions.

Pigs

Draw the oval and small circle. Sketch in the legs and hooves.

Finish it as usual, adding the tail and the black spots.

Pigs are good-natured.

You can make them do many things that people do.

Of course, they wouldn't run in this crazy way, but they look funnier.

Wild Hogs

The razorback hog lives in the southeastern part of the United States. They roam in the woods in a half-wild state.

European wild boars are hunted all over Europe.

African warthog

In the southwestern states the peccary (sometimes called javelina) can be found. This is the smallest of the wild pigs.

Goats

Finish it as shown. Goats are hairy animals. Make use of this fact.

Draw two ovals of different sizes. Then sketch in the beard, horns, tail, legs, and hooves.

The so-called mountain goat is not really a goat. It belongs to the antelope family.

Goats like to climb.

19

Sheep

Finish it with big split hooves and slender legs. Give the sheep a woolly look with the wiggly lines.

Draw two ovals for the head and body. Sketch in the ears, tail, legs, and feet.

Mountain sheep, or the bighorn, have large and beautiful horns. They are graceful and sure-footed.

Lambs are easy to draw. Skinny legs and a large, fat tail are common.

Chickens and Ducks

Draw two circles as shown above.

Finish the head. Add the tail, wing, comb, and feet.

Good morning!

The family

Start with two ovals.

Finish the head. Put in the neck, wing, tail, and feet. Black it in.

A nice day for a swim

Wild Birds

Draw the two ovals.

Finish it, and put in the solid black.

Just a bird

Pelican

Vulture

Cranes have long and long necks.

Birds' beaks differ.

Birds in flight

Fish

Start with a leaf shape.

Finish like this.

They can be thin or fat.

Whale

Deep-sea monster

Shark

Porpoises

Fish are all shapes.

Deer and Moose

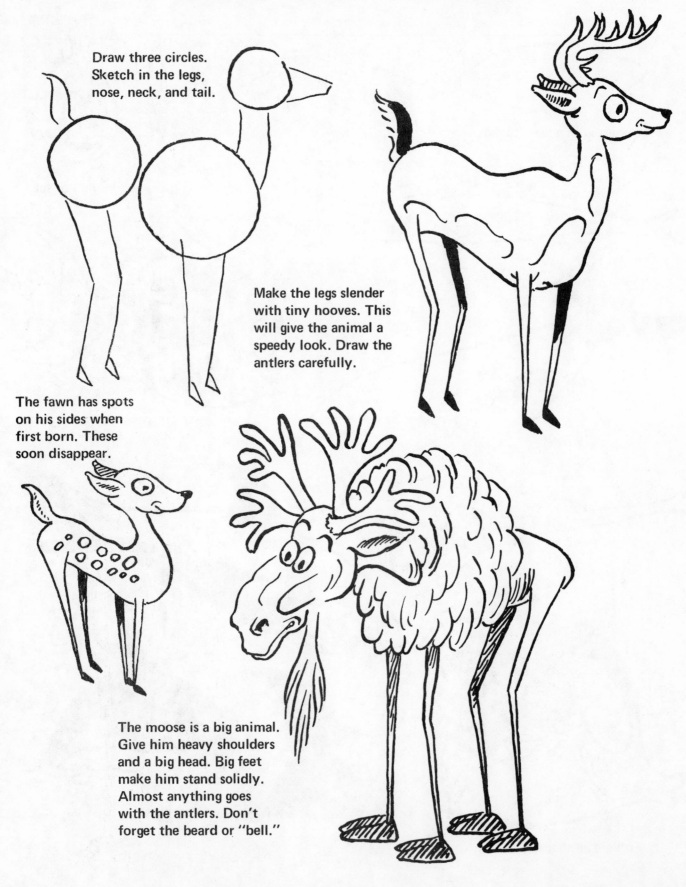

Draw three circles. Sketch in the legs, nose, neck, and tail.

Make the legs slender with tiny hooves. This will give the animal a speedy look. Draw the antlers carefully.

The fawn has spots on his sides when first born. These soon disappear.

The moose is a big animal. Give him heavy shoulders and a big head. Big feet make him stand solidly. Almost anything goes with the antlers. Don't forget the beard or "bell."

Antelopes and Giraffe

Draw a circle and an oval. Sketch in the nose, neck, legs, and tail.

American antelope, commonly called the pronghorn.

Slender legs and streamlined body give an alert look.

This is not a full-grown giraffe. The adults have much longer legs and necks. Note the odd tail. Big hooves give a solid look.

The African gazelle is fast and graceful.

Bears

Start with a circle and a large oval. Sketch in the nose, legs, and tail.

Bears look heavy and clumsy. Finish in the usual way. Add rough coat, thick legs, and big feet. Don't forget the long claws.

Cubs are playful

This one is in a big hurry.

The polar bear has a longer neck and body than his cousins.

Bears vary in size, from the big Alaskan Kodiak bear to the small black bear in Florida.

Monkeys

Draw two circles and an oval. Sketch in the arms and legs.

Finish it. Add the ears, features, and tail.

Draw monkeys with human faces.

Make the arms longer than the legs.

Apes

These three are the main big apes.

Draw three ovals. Sketch in the arms and legs.

The gorilla is a big hulking animal. Draw him with heavy arms and legs. The head jams right into the body. He has no neck.

The orangutan is about two-thirds as large as the gorilla.

The chimpanzee is very intelligent. It is smaller than the gorilla.

Frogs-Turtles-Lizards

Draw two ovals.

Add the face, legs, and feet. Put in the black spots.

Lizards are like small dinosaurs.

Turtles are fun to draw. Have fun with the shell markings.

Kangaroos

Draw a small circle and the two ovals as shown. Add the nose, ears, legs, and feet.

Draw in the long feet and tail. Finish it as shown.

"Now for the record high jump!"

Mom and baby

Walruses-Seals

The walrus is a huge beast sometimes weighing a ton or more. He's all wrinkles and whiskers. Long tusks help when digging for clams and other shell fish.

Two ovals make the basic shape. Add the tusks and flippers.

Seals and sea lions are very clever. They can be taught many amusing tricks. Baby seals are fat and well-fed.

Lions

Start with two ovals and a leaf shape. Then add the legs, feet, and tail.

The most important feature of the male lion is the mane.

The lioness has no mane. Otherwise, she is very much like the lion.

HI COUSIN

Lions are related to cats, only they are larger.

Tigers-Leopards

Draw a circle and a leaf shape. Draw the legs, feet, and tail.

Now finish the tiger. Big feet, big claws, and stripes help.

The leopard has spots instead of stripes. You can use dots, squares, triangles, or any other shapes. It will still look like a leopard.

33

Rhinos-Hippos

Draw two circles and an oval.
Sketch the legs, horn, and big feet.

Finish it. Put in the features
and add the ears and toenails.

Rhinos and hippos have
about the same body shape.

When a hippo
yawns, he really
means it.

34